I Can Taste

Julie Murray

Abdo
SENSES
Kids

abdopublishing.com

Published by Abdo Kids, a division of ABDO, PO Box 398166, Minneapolis, Minnesota 55439.
Copyright © 2016 by Abdo Consulting Group, Inc. International copyrights reserved in all countries.
No part of this book may be reproduced in any form without written permission from the publisher.

Printed in the United States of America, North Mankato, Minnesota.

052015

092015

 THIS BOOK CONTAINS
RECYCLED MATERIALS

Photo Credits: Glow Images, iStock, Shutterstock

Production Contributors: Teddy Borth, Jennie Forsberg, Grace Hansen

Design Contributors: Candice Keimig, Dorothy Toth

Library of Congress Control Number: 2014958413

Cataloging-in-Publication Data

Murray, Julie.
 I can taste / Julie Murray.
   p. cm. -- (Senses)
ISBN 978-1-62970-928-4
Includes index.
1. Taste--Juvenile literature.   I. Title.
612.8'7--dc23
                        2014958413

DEC. 24 2015

Table of Contents

I Can Taste 4

The Five Senses 22

Glossary. 23

Index 24

Abdo Kids Code. 24

I Can Taste

There are five senses.

Taste is one of the senses.

We taste with our mouths.

We taste things every day!

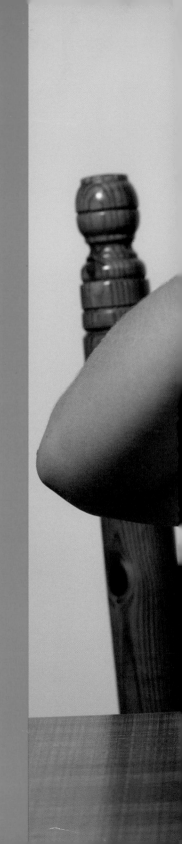

We taste sweet things.

Max eats cake.

We taste **sour** things.

Ella eats a lemon.

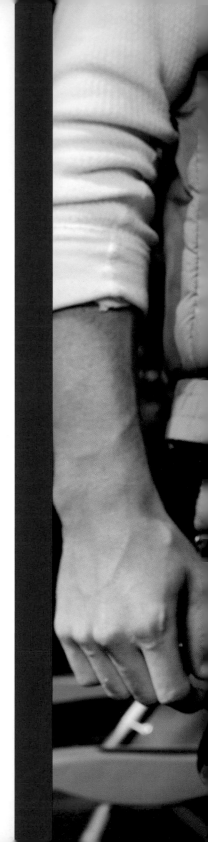

We taste 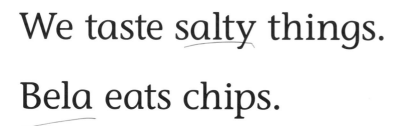salty things.

Bela eats chips.

We taste **spicy** things.

Eve eats tacos.

We taste hot things.

Avi eats soup.

We taste cold things.

Mila eats ice cream.

What did you taste today?

The Five Senses

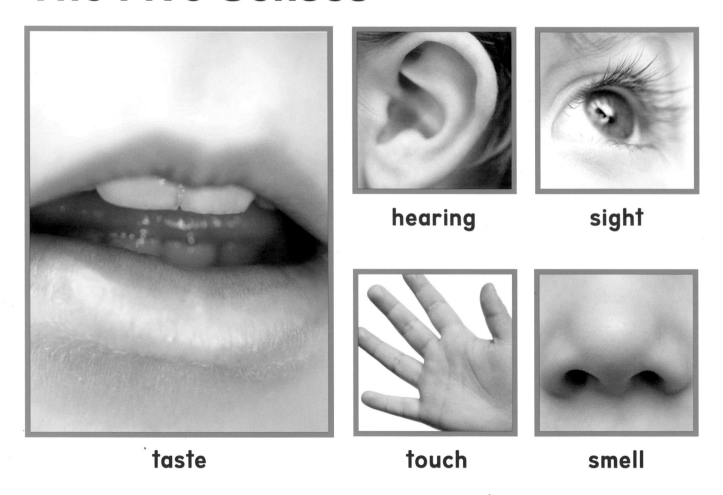

taste

hearing

sight

touch

smell

Glossary

sour
a food with a sharp taste.
Lemons are sour.

spicy
a food flavored with or having
strong spices. Spicy foods can leave
a burning feeling in your mouth.

Index

cold 18

hot 16

mouth 6

salty 12

senses 4

sour 10

spicy 14

sweet 8

abdokids.com

Use this code to log on to abdokids.com and access crafts, games, videos, and more!

Abdo Kids Code:
SIK9284